Brain Waves

Tudor Times

Christine Moorcroft

Contents

Introduction	3	Tudor music	28
Teachers' notes	4	Dance: 'Gathering peascods'	29
Travel back in time	9	At the table	30
The Tudor Rose	10	Tudor recipe: cheese tart	31
Tudor family tree	11	On the roads	32
Henry VIII	12	At sea	33
Catherine of Aragon	13	Adventurers and traders	34
Towns	14	Sea routes	35
The country	15	The quarrel with Spain	36
Tudors at work – in towns	16	The Spanish Armada	37
Tudors at work – the farmer's wife	17	Printing: Tudor bestsellers	38
Vagrants	18	Going to school in 1557	39
The break with Rome	19	Shovelboard	40
Closing the monasteries	20	Sports and games	41
Thomas More	21	A manor house	42
Edward VI	22	The great chamber	43
Mary 1	23	An ordinary home	44
Elizabeth I	24	Keeping healthy	45
Bess of Hardwick	25	Clothes for a nobleman (1500)	46–47
Mary, Queen of Scots	26	A Tudor comedy	48
Entertaining the Queen	27		

Acknowledgements

The author wishes to thank Keith Scott for his assistance with research and Lord Petre for permission to copy the plans of Ingatestone Hall.

Folens allows photocopying of pages marked 'copiable page' for educational use, providing that this use is within the confines of the purchasing institution. Copiable pages should not be declared in any return in respect of any photocopying licence.

Folens books are protected by international copyright laws. All rights are reserved. The copyright of all materials in this book, except where otherwise stated, remains the property of the publisher and author. No part of this publication may be reproduced, stored in a retrieval system, or transmitted, in any form or by any means, for whatever purpose, without the written permission of Folens Limited.

This resource may be used in a variety of ways. However, it is not intended that teachers or children should write directly into the book itself.

Christine Moorcroft hereby asserts her moral rights to be identified as the author of this work in accordance with the Copyright, Designs and Patents Act 1988.

Editor: Edward Rippeth
Illustrations: Bob Farley (Graham-Cameron Illustrations)
Cover design: Hybert Design & Type
Layout artist: Patricia Hollingsworth
Cover image: Bridgeman Art Library

© 1996 Folens Limited, on behalf of the author.
Every effort has been made to contact copyright holders of material used in this book. If any have been overlooked, we will be pleased to make any necessary arrangements.

First published 1996 by Folens Limited, Dunstable and Dublin.
Folens Limited, Albert House, Apex Business Centre, Boscombe Road, Dunstable LU5 4RL, England.

ISBN 1 85276 892-4

Introduction

Brain Waves: Tudor Times provides activity sheets to support existing resources, for example *Folens A Time to Remember: Tudor Times*. It complements *Folens Ideas Bank: Tudor Times*. The activity sheets help children to find out about some of the major personalities of the time, including monarchs, major events and the way of life of people in town and country and at different levels of society.

Most of the activities can be carried out without any extra source material. For those that require research on the part of the children, the teachers' notes on pages 4–8 give details of resources required. These notes suggest ways to introduce and enhance the activities, including use of local sources: museums, sites, records, art galleries, copies of works of art.

The wide range of sources shown across the activities provides children with opportunities to find out about the period using, for example, literature and art from the time, inventories, letters, accounts and journals.

The material is presented in a way that does not make judgements about people or events, but encourages the children to do this.

The National Curriculum states that children should be taught about arts and architecture, including Shakespeare, but virtually all of the material that this book is designed to complement covers Shakespeare. 'A Tudor comedy' (page 48) presents a broader view of the theatre by developing awareness of the other dramatists who were active at the time.

Some of the activities are designed to show the positive role of women in Tudor times, for example, Bess of Hardwick, who used the systems of marriage contracts and inheritance to found a great dynasty. Henry VIII's divorce is shown from the point of view of Catherine of Aragon, so that children can appreciate her strength of character. The role of the farmer's wife, although her title suggests subservience, is shown to be one that involves considerable skill, responsibility and power.

Brain Waves: Tudor Times addresses the key elements of History in the National Curriculum for Key Stage 2 as follows:

	Key elements	Activities
Chronology	People and changes within a chronological framework	9, 10, 11, 13, 22, 25, 26
	Dates and terms relating to the passage of time	9, 10
Range and depth of historical knowledge/ understanding	Characteristics of particular period	14, 15, 16, 17, 18, 27, 28, 29, 30, 31, 32, 38, 39, 40, 41, 46-47
	Reasons for, and results of, historical events, situations, changes	19, 20, 21, 23, 24, 36, 37, 41
	Links between main events, situations, changes within and across periods	10, 14, 16
Historical inquiry	Finding out about aspects of the period, using sources	12, 17, 18, 30, 31, 32, 34, 40, 42, 45, 48
	Asking/answering questions/ selecting/recording information	39, 43, 44
Organisation and communication	Recalling/selecting/organising historical information	45
	Communicating knowledge & understanding of history	All activities

Teachers' notes

Travel back in time — Page 9
Encourage the children to notice the distances on the time line between events in Tudor times and between Tudor times and the present day. Enlarge and extend the time line to allow the children to relate their knowledge of other ages in history with Tudor times.

The Tudor Rose — Page 10
Ask the children about badges that they wear. Which ones show that they belong to or support a group or organisation? What was symbolised by the Tudor Rose? Draw attention to the reasons for royal marriages in Tudor times. The children could compare these with royal marriages of other times in history, including the present day.

Tudor family tree — Page 11
The rules for succession to the throne are complex. A male heir was preferred over a female heir, regardless of age. Edward VI succeeded Henry VIII as his eldest son. If Edward had married and had children, they would have succeeded him. Instead he was succeeded by Mary I, his eldest sister, and because she had no heirs, Elizabeth I, his other sister, was next.

Henry VIII — Page 12
Page 11 is needed for reference.
Ask the children what they can find out about Henry VIII from the letter and speech. The text tells them that he was married to Catherine of Aragon. Henry was concerned that he had no male heir. He says that his marriage 'was against God's law', referring to the fact that Catherine had been the wife of his dead elder brother, Arthur. The evidence suggests that he wanted to marry Anne Boleyn so that he might have a son, and the letter shows his affection for her.
Source of the speech and letter: *English Historical Documents, Volume V, 1485-1558* (Eyre and Spottiswoode).

Catherine of Aragon — Page 13
The activity presents Henry VIII's divorce from Catherine of Aragon's point of view. She insisted that her marriage to Henry was legal because her marriage to Arthur had never been consummated. After the divorce Henry gave her the title Princess Dowager, but she insisted that as his lawful wife she was still Queen of England. Many years later, Eustace Chapuys, an emissary of Henry VIII, described Catherine as one of the most virtuous women he had ever known and the highest-hearted. Thomas Cromwell, Secretary of State to Henry VIII is quoted as having said that she 'might have surpassed all the heroes of history' had she been a man (*Tudor Women*, by Alison Plowden, Weidenfeld and Nicolson).

Towns — Page 14
Drawings, descriptions and statutes from the time tell us that large towns were unhealthy places because residents threw rubbish, including human waste, into the streets. The presence of horses and sometimes cattle and sheep added to the general filth (see *English Historical Documents*, op cit, for records of laws that were passed in order to keep towns clean). Local record offices may have similar records for your area. The children should notice the different causes of pollution in present day towns and could find out about recent laws designed to reduce it. They could research bye-laws of a local town to find out how these problems are tackled. There were attempts in Tudor times to 'clean up' towns, for example, in Winchester in 1523, people were required to clean the streets adjoining their houses and gardens. The fine for non-compliance was 6s. 8d. A Mr Gilbert of Winchester was recorded, in *The Black Book of Winchester*, as having his fine waived in return for cleaning all the windows of the Council building.

Teachers' notes

The country — Page 15
It is easy to assume that the problems of agriculture were caused by the enclosure of common land to provide grazing for sheep. Joan Thirsk suggests, in *Tudor Enclosures* (Historical Association), that this oversimplifies things. A study of the London food market shows that there was much local specialisation in food production in England, and enclosures took place in different forms, varying in character from one part of the country to another.

The mediaeval strip farming system which continued into Tudor times was often disorganised. Villagers sometimes sowed or ploughed the wrong strip by mistake. Some did not look after their land, leaving their successors with a difficult task. If landlords 'engrossed' (combined two or more farms), farmers were left homeless. When a tenant farmer died the landlord often forced his family to leave by increasing the rent.

Tudors at work – in towns — Page 16
Encourage the children to use dictionaries to find the meanings of unfamiliar words. They could approach this task by beginning with some of the occupations seen in present-day towns. Which ones were found in Tudor times? Can they explain their answers?

Tudors at work – the farmer's wife — Page 17
Encourage the children to consider the hard work of the farmer's wife and her responsibility and authority in the running of the farm. She would be responsible for buying and selling in the market and obtaining the best prices. She would often have complete charge of all the household and farm accounts.
Source: *English Historical Documents, op cit.*

Vagrants — Page 18
William Harrison in his *Description of England*, written in the 1570s, described poor people as belonging to three groups: 'the impotent poor' (lame, blind, incurably ill and orphans), 'poor by casualty' (wounded soldiers) and the 'thriftless poor'. In London the first two groups, deemed 'the deserving poor' were helped by four institutions; Bethlehem or Bedlam for the insane, St Bartholomew's Hospital for the sick, Christ's Hospital for children and St Thomas' for the aged and infirm. Bridewell, once a royal palace, was a house of correction and training for the 'thriftless poor'.

Sources: Acts of Parliament, i) for the provision and relief of the poor (1552), ii) Act for the relief of the poor (1555) in *English Historical Documents, op cit.*

The break with Rome — Page 19
Although he wanted a divorce from Catherine of Aragon, Henry VIII did not immediately break away from the Roman Church. He was essentially a Roman Catholic, not a Protestant, and only left the Church when it became politically necessary. It would be easy to assume that people would welcome church services, a prayer book and Bible in a language that they understood, but it should be remembered that there are always people who will resist changes in things that they value.

Closing the monasteries — Page 20
Draw attention to the reasons that Henry VIII gave for closing the monasteries, for example, idleness and corruption among monks and friars. The king gained much valuable land once owned by religious orders. He sold much of this property to members of the court. The closure of the monasteries caused problems. There was less help for poor people, who received alms at monasteries, less education for children of the less well off, and large numbers of displaced monks and nuns. Many of the monks and nuns were pleased to take up new occupations if they could. Others fought to regain the monasteries.

Thomas More — Page 21
Ask the children to think of people who stuck to their principles or faith, despite it being dangerous for them. They may be familiar with stories of faith leaders and saints. Thomas More was canonised by the Catholic Church. Ask the children to explain what More did that led to his death.

Edward VI — Page 22
The children should notice that Edward VI was a child when he became king. The game draws attention to the struggle for power between the Dukes of Somerset and Northumberland that came about because the king was too young to rule alone. Evidence suggests that Edward, although young, had a very good grasp of affairs of state, and read all the official papers.

Teachers' notes

Mary I — Page 23
This activity draws attention to the continuing religious struggle throughout the Tudor period. Ask the children how the ordinary people of the time might have felt. Nearly 300 priests and bishops were burned at the stake during Mary's reign.

Source: 'Acts and Monuments' (*The Book of Martyrs* by John Fox, 1563). This is a record of all who were killed in the name of religion during Mary's reign.

Elizabeth I — Page 24
Ask the children to explain why Elizabeth's advisers were keen to find a husband for her. Discuss how the course of history might have been changed if Elizabeth had married Phillip II of Spain (this could be done in conjunction with page 37, 'The Spanish Armada').

Bess of Hardwick — Page 25
Bess of Hardwick was remarkable in that she lived far longer than most of her contemporaries. She began with no property, the daughter of a fairly wealthy country squire, whose land and home could not be inherited by his family because his eldest son was under the age of majority. A legal agreement, common at the time, meant that such property reverted to the crown. After an early marriage and widowhood, Bess proceeded to secure some extremely useful marriage contracts. The dynasty that she founded continues today. The present Duke of Devonshire is her descendant. Bess' story reveals much about marriage arrangements in Tudor times. Useful sources: archives and displays at Hardwick Hall, Chesterfield.

Mary, Queen of Scots — Page 26
It was feared at the time that Mary, Queen of Scots, might gather support to claim the English throne, because she was the grand-daughter of Margaret Tudor, sister of Henry VIII. Mary was behind a great deal of plotting, but Elizabeth I's spies were active in ensuring that nothing came of it. Evidence suggests that Elizabeth I was very upset at having to sign the warrant for Mary's execution, although it was for her own safety. The connection between Mary, Queen of Scots, and Bess of Hardwick was that Bess (by then Countess of Shrewsbury) and her husband were asked to guard Mary. She lived with them for about eleven years. Bess' daughter, Elizabeth Cavendish, married Charles Stuart, Mary's uncle.

Entertaining the Queen — Page 27
The 'progresses' or journeys of Elizabeth I and her court are well-documented. Ask the children why wealthy people left London in the summer. Elizabeth made a famous visit to Kenilworth Castle, where she was entertained extravagantly by the Earl of Leicester. The expense of such a visit, by the Queen and hundreds of courtiers, was borne by the host. Preparations for such a visit included a complete spring cleaning of the house, new rushes on the floor, banquets and other meals for the visitors, and entertainment, such as music, dancing, a play and sometimes an elaborate pageant.

Tudor music — Page 28
Collect and display copies of works of art from the time, showing musical instruments. Can the children recognise any? Some are similar to instruments used today, but others will be unfamiliar. The game is designed to encourage the children to look closely at each. If possible, play recordings of these instruments.

Dance: 'Gathering peascods' — Page 29
The instructions for this dance are simplified from 'The Dancing Master', published in 1665. The book provides a collection of music and dances from the preceding century and more. The children could begin and end the dance with a bow or curtsey to their partners. The original music was as follows:

At the table — Page 30
Provide works of art from the time showing people seated at meal tables. Ask the children what people ate with and from. Forks were not introduced (from Italy) until the end of Elizabeth I's reign. People usually had their own knives for eating, kept in small bags hanging at their waists. They ate many items with their fingers, hence the 'aquamanile' or finger bowl. The elaborately designed salt cellars held salt in a hollow. The small hollow on the wooden trenchers (plates) was for salt. Until Tudor times trenchers consisted of thick, hard slices of bread.

Useful sources: Portrait of Sir Henry Unton and family (National Portrait Gallery); Portrait of Lord Cobham and his family, owned by the Marquis of Bath, Longleat, Wilts, and reproduced in many history text books; *A Fete at Bermondsey* by Joris Hoefnagel, at Hatfield House, Herts, owned by the Marquis of Salisbury.

Teachers' notes

Tudor recipe: cheese tart — Page 31
Provide works of art and descriptions of meals of the time. Ask the children to list any unfamiliar or unusual foods. Ask them to explain the absence of some common foods that people eat today. They should notice that foods from overseas were beginning to appear in England in Tudor times, for example pineapples, potatoes and bananas.

On the roads — Page 32
The children should notice, from the sources provided, that responsibility for the upkeep of roads fell on those living near them. Roads had deteriorated since they were made in Roman times. It may be possible to find local records providing evidence of how roads in your locality were maintained.

At sea — Page 33
This activity helps the children to find out about how ships were navigated and powered. One of the main problems in navigating was the lack of accurate chronometers, without which it was difficult to measure longitude precisely using star charts. Hourglasses were used, but were not precise. One instrument still used in navigating is the sextant.

Adventurers and traders / Sea routes — Page 34/35
Begin with a collection of food wrappers. Ask the children to list the ingredients. Do they know which are produced in Britain and which are imported? Draw attention to the difference that overseas traders made to the lives of many people. They could write an account of the reaction of a Tudor family to unfamiliar goods seen for the first time.
Before Tudor times, English monarchs had been occupied with defending the crown. With Henry VII came peace and stability.
Other European countries had established overseas trade routes long before England and had begun to found colonies in the West Indies and America. Unexplored routes could be found by travelling north, which was one of the reasons why Anthony Jenkinson and others sailed to Russia and tried to establish trade there. Use the map for the children to draw Jenkinson's route through Russia to Turkey. They could add the routes of the better known explorers such as Francis Drake, John Hawkins and John and Sebastian Cabot.

The quarrel with Spain — Page 36
Provide maps and reference books that help the children to find out more about the quarrel between England and Spain. The people and quotations should be matched as follows:
1. Pope Sixtus, 2. William Cecil (Lord Burghley),
3. Phillip II of Spain, 4. The Earl of Leicester,
5. Elizabeth I, 6. Francis Drake.

The Spanish Armada — Page 37
This activity encourages the children to consider evidence and make their own judgements as to the reason why Phillip II of Spain attacked England with the Spanish Armada. Provide pictures of the types of ships used and works of art that record scenes from the battles.

Printing: Tudor bestsellers — Page 38
Before the invention of the printing press manuscripts were copied by hand, usually by monks. Printing meant that books were quicker to produce and more widely available. During the reign of Elizabeth I there was an enormous increase in the number of books produced and sold, and in the number of people who could read. The titles of some of the books shown on the activity sheet show that people from different levels of society, not only scholars and the rich, could read.

Going to school in 1557 — Page 39
Most learning had taken place in monasteries, and their dissolution meant that many schools closed. However, during the reign of Henry VIII, many new schools were founded. Monks continued to teach, but the separate profession of schoolmaster (all were men) was emerging. Children of the gentry learned to read at home until the age of seven, then boys could attend grammar schools until the age of fifteen and some went on to university. There is evidence that some grammar schools provided, in their surrounding parishes, 'grammarians' who taught children of all social backgrounds to read to the minimum standard for entry to the schools. Girls were generally taught reading and the skills thought necessary for running a household.
The children could use reference books to find out about the subjects taught to boys and girls. Can they explain these differences? How did Tudor education differ from their own? Several publications addressed to schoolchildren and those who taught them have survived from Tudor times. The source of this extract is *The Schoole of Vertue* by A.F. Seager (1557).

Teachers' notes

Shovelboard — Page 40
'Shovelboard' is an ancestor of 'shove halfpenny'. Board and card games were popular in Tudor times, but, as shown on page 41, Henry VIII's parliament passed rules to discourage them, because it was thought that if men played these games they would have less time for archery. Archery was an important skill for men at the time, who could be called upon to defend the nation.

Sports and games — Page 41
Ask the children about price regulations and subsidies which are used to influence what people spend their money on. Examples include lead-free fuel and nuclear power. By regulating the price of longbows men were encouraged to buy them, so that they would use them in archery. This would improve their skills as soldiers.

A manor house — Page 42
Ingatestone Hall is a typical Tudor manor house, but its water supply and drainage systems were very modern for the time. It was rare for any houses to have toilets with a water supply. Most had draughty mediaeval garderobes, which consisted of a hole in the floor above a pit, often in a turret. Toilets were known by many euphemisms including 'houses of office', 'stool houses', 'privvies' and 'jakes'. The accounts of Ingatestone Hall contain a bill for two shillings for 'cleaning the jakes about the house'. The great chamber, shown on page 43, was a feature of Tudor manor houses. The other notable feature, on the first floor, was a long gallery, where the occupants and their guests would walk, talk and listen to music. Servants tended to sleep downstairs, sometimes in passageways, so that they could be called upon if needed (Mistress Keble was the housekeeper). The family and their guests slept upstairs. Butter and beer were usually made on the premises. Wine and beer would be stored in readiness for guests. The house, like other manor houses, had an armoury, since all gentlemen were expected to be ready to fight for their country if needed.
Source: *Tudor Food and Pastimes: Life at Ingatestone Hall* by F.G.Emmison (Ernest Benn, 1964).

The great chamber — Page 43
If possible, visit a Tudor manor house and/or provide pictures showing the interior. Ask the children to list the furniture used at the time and to notice what it was made from. They should notice that, in general, there was little furniture and that ornately carved wood was popular. Carpets were rarely put on floors. They were used to cover tables and as wall hangings. Floors were covered with rushes or woven rush mats.

An ordinary home — Page 44
The home of Alexander Paramore is a typical village house belonging to a fairly prosperous farmer. The children should notice how sparsely furnished it is. A 'painted cloth' replaces the carpets of the manor house. Often, only adults were seated while eating. Children would stand at the table. Cooking took place at large open fires in the kitchen and hall. Water would be brought from a well. It can be seen that the second bedroom was also used as a store room.

Tudor homes are often assumed to have been unhygienic places, a view supported by some sources from the time. Erasmus wrote about the filth that accumulated in the rushes that was never removed, merely covered with fresh rushes from time to time. However, household accounts show that rushes were frequently swept out and replaced.
Sources: *Life in Tudor England*, Penry Williams, Batsford, 1964; *Elizabethan Life in Town and Country*, M. St Clare Byrne, Methuen, 1961; *How They Lived: 1485–1700*, M. Harrison and O.M.Royston, Basil Blackwell, 1963.

Keeping healthy — Page 45
The children should notice the differences between then and now, and that experts during Tudor times often gave conflicting advice about health, just as they do today.
Sources: see notes for page 44.

Clothes for a nobleman (1500) — Pages 46–47
Space prohibits the inclusion of clothes for women, children and people from different social groups. Works of art and effigies on tombs are invaluable sources of information about costume. Discuss the changes in fashion during Tudor times, from the early example shown on the activity sheet. The children could produce Tudor fashion time lines for men and women. Children were generally dressed as adults, boys wearing dresses until the age of about five.

A Tudor comedy — Page 48
Use other sources to introduce the Tudor theatre and Shakespeare. There were many other dramatists, and some of their plays could be simplified for the children to read (note that some are rather bawdy in their humour because this was what people enjoyed!).
Source: *Six Plays by Contemporaries of Shakespeare*, Oxford University Press, 1958.

Travel back in time

The time line shows when the Tudors lived.

- What year is it now?

  _____

- On the time line, mark this in red.

- Add an extra box to the time line to show when you were born.

- Find out the dates of birth of these people:

Your mother, father or person who looks after you	
One of your grandparents	
The oldest person you know	

- Find out the dates of some events that interest you.

Event	Date

- Make an enlarged copy of the time line so that you can add these.

- As you learn more about the Tudors, add more dates to your enlarged time line.

1485 Henry VII became the first Tudor monarch.

1588 Elizabeth I's ships defeated the Spanish Armada.

1603 Elizabeth I, the last Tudor monarch, died.

1901 Sarah Johnson, the grandmother of the author of this book, was born.

1949 Christine Moorcroft, the author of this book, was born.

1450 — 1500 — 1550 — 1600 — 1650 — 1700 — 1750 — 1800 — 1850 — 1900 — 1950 — 2000

© Folens (copiable page)   BRAIN WAVES – Tudor Times

The Tudor Rose

For 30 years before Henry VII became king, two branches of the royal family had been fighting for the throne.

Lancaster
Henry Tudor

York
Richard III

Henry Tudor defeated Richard III at the Battle of Bosworth in 1485. He married Elizabeth of York and he made a new family badge from the white rose of York and the red rose of Lancaster.

He called it the Tudor Rose.

- Colour this rose to show how this could be done.

People can be rivals for many things, such as a football competition or political power. They often have coloured badges or symbols.

- Name two rival groups

  _____ and _____

- In Box A draw and colour a new badge to show friendship between the two groups.

Box A

Tudor family tree

- Who was Henry VIII's father? _____
- Who was his mother? _____
- Who was Henry VII's grandson? _____

Families often have their own coat of arms, like the Tudors' shown here.

Key: = married
r. reigned

Arthur (died 1502) = **1.** Catherine of Aragon

Henry VII = Elizabeth of York
r. 1485–1509

Henry VIII = **2.** Anne Boleyn

Mary Margaret
Henry VIII = **3.** Jane Seymour
4. Anne of Cleves
5. Catherine Howard
6. Catherine Parr
r. 1509–1547

Mary I = Phillip of Spain
r. 1553–1558

Elizabeth I
r. 1558–1603

Edward VI
r. 1547–1553

- In what order did Henry VIII's children reign?
  1. _____
  2. _____
  3. _____
- Explain this order to a friend.

Now

- Here is another Tudor family.

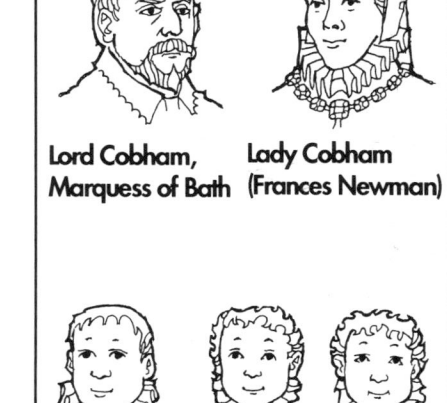

Lord Cobham, Marquess of Bath   Lady Cobham (Frances Newman)

Maximillian Henry William

Elizabeth Frances Margeret

- Draw their family tree on a separate sheet of paper.

Henry VIII

Use sources **A** and **B**, box **C** and the Tudor family tree to help you answer the questions.

A

"... if it be determined by judgement that our marriage was against God's law and clearly void, then I shall ... sorrow the departing from such a good lady ... and bewail my unfortunate chance that I have ... no true heir of my body to inherit this realm."

A. Henry VIII said this in 1528 about his marriage to Catherine of Aragon.

Glossary

bewail	– be sorry about
determined	– decided
heir	– person who takes over when person dies
inherit	– take over when someone dies
void	– against the law

B

"The proofs of your affection are such... that I am obliged to love, honour and serve you truly for ever ...
... wishing the time short and thinking it long until we two meet again ...
   Your loyal and most assured servant
      H seeks AB and no other R."

B. Henry VIII wrote this in a letter to Anne Boleyn between 1527–1528.

C

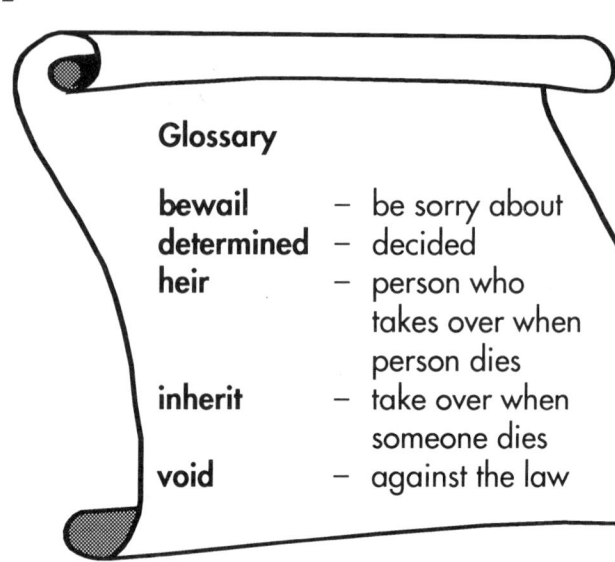

Catherine of Aragon married Arthur, elder brother of Henry VIII, in 1501. Arthur died in 1502. Catherine married Henry VIII in 1509. Henry divorced her and married Anne Boleyn.

Henry VIII   **Anne Boleyn**

Catherine of Aragon

- List three possible reasons for Henry's divorce from Catherine.

  1. _____
  2. _____
  3. _____

- Circle the reason that Henry gave for the divorce.

- Which do you think was the true reason? _____

- Explain your answer to a friend.

Catherine of Aragon

- Read Catherine of Aragon's story.
- Write in the 'thought bubbles' how you think Catherine felt.

Catherine's parents were King Ferdinand and Queen Isabella of Spain. They planned for her to marry Arthur, the son of Henry VII of England. Arthur was fourteen and Catherine was fifteen when they married in 1501.

Six months later Arthur died. Henry VII wanted to stay friendly with Spain. His younger son, Henry, married Catherine. Henry became King Henry VIII in 1509.

In 1516 Catherine gave birth to Princess Mary. Her other sons and daughters died when they were babies. Henry wanted a son to become the next king of England.

In about 1524 Henry VIII fell in love with Anne Boleyn. He wanted to divorce Catherine. The Pope did not give permission for this so Henry made himself head of the Church in England and married Anne Boleyn.

- **NOW** • Find out what became of Catherine of Aragon after the divorce.

Towns

- Talk to a friend about the differences and similarities between these pictures.

A town in Tudor times.   A present-day town.

- List the things that make towns unpleasant.

Tudor town	Present-day town
_____	_____
_____	_____
_____	_____
_____	_____
_____	_____

NOW
- Find out what was done to try to improve towns:
  – in Tudor times
  – in the present day.

The country

Many people earned a living by farming the land of rich landlords. The land around a village (common land) was often divided into strips which were worked by the villagers.

To give everyone a turn on the best land they swapped strips every one or two years.

Some farmers owned their farms. Yeomen farmers rented their farms from rich landlords.

In Tudor times farming changed.

- Match the speech bubbles to the people.

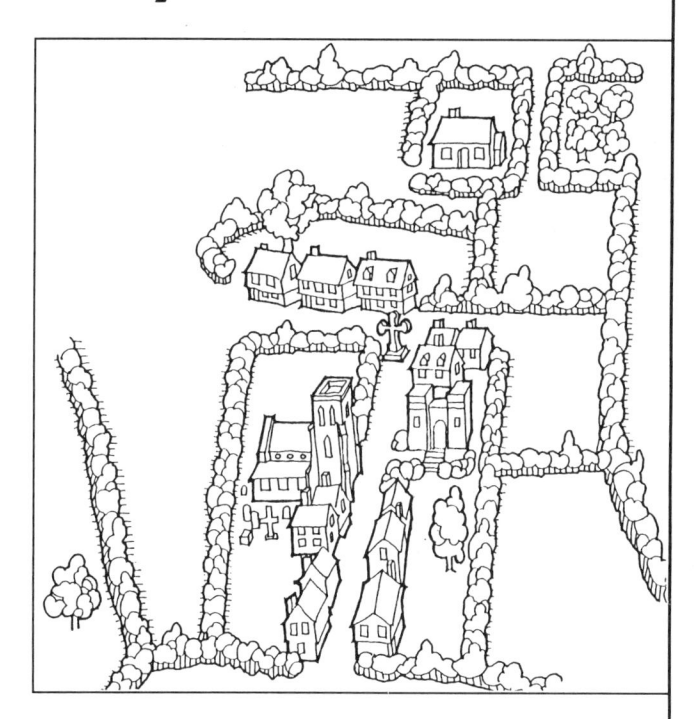

A landlord

A villager

It might be easier for me to farm five strips of land enclosed into one field.

What will happen to me if the landlord joins these two farms? He will want only one farmer.

If I fence in the common land I can keep my own sheep on it.

If the farmer changes from crops to sheep, he will need fewer workers. I might have no job.

A yeoman farmer

A farm worker paid by a farmer

NOW
- Imagine you are a Tudor villager.
- Write a letter to a friend in a town discussing what is happening in your village.

© Folens (copiable page)   BRAIN WAVES – Tudor Times

Tudors at work – in towns

Look at the pictures to find out about work in Tudor towns.

- Complete the chart to show how work in towns has changed since Tudor times.

1. Town crier

2. Rat catcher

Picture	Do we still see this?	What we see today.

3. Water carrier 
4. Laundress 
5. Shoemaker 
6. Goldsmith

- Find out what a town crier used to do. List his jobs.

- Explain why towns today do not need town criers.

7. Parish constable

8. Cooper

Tudors at work – the farmer's wife

Read this description of a day's work of a Tudor farmer's wife. It is from *The Book of Husbandry*, written in 1523.

The glossary will help.

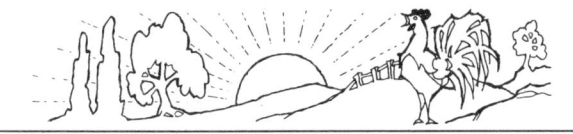

Glossary

array	– dress
kye	– cow
meat	– food
ordain	– send
Pater Noster	– a prayer
swine	– pigs
syc up	– strain

'First in a morning when thou art waked lift up thine hand and bless thee, and make a sign of the holy cross ... say a Pater Noster ... then first sweep thy house, dress up thy dishboard and set all things in good order: milk thy kye, ... syc up thy milk, take up thy children and array them and provide for thy husband's breakfast, dinner and supper ... ordain corn and malt to the mill, to bake and brew withal when need is...and see that thou have thy measure again...or else the miller dealeth not truly with thee. Thou must make butter and cheese...serve thy swine both morning and evening, and give thy poultry meat in the morning.'

The farmer's wife usually sold eggs, milk, corn, vegetables and poultry at the market. She used the money to buy whatever was needed.

- Make a timetable for a farmer's wife's day

Time	Activity
6.00	Wake up
6.05	Say the Lord's Prayer

- What skills did a farmer's wife need?

- Write a day's timetable of a woman you know. Describe her whole day from getting up to going to bed. Compare it with the Tudor farmer's wife's day.

March

Planting herbs and vegetables, weeding.

April

Spinning flax.

May

Spinning wool, making clothes, malting, helping to make hay, reap corn and help with all farm work.

Vagrants

Vagrants wandered around towns begging. Parliament passed some laws to help vagrants.

Some beggars had licences to beg. They could only beg in certain areas.

Any able-bodied person aged fourteen or over found begging could be whipped.

Minstrels were punished as vagrants unless they worked for a noble householder or a town.

Some people pretended to have fits. They put foaming mixtures in their mouths. They pretended to be mentally ill.

- List some reasons why people might have become vagrants, for example, blindness.

  _____ _____
  _____ _____
  _____ _____
  _____

- Why did some able-bodied vagrants pretend to have fits? _____
  _____
  _____
  _____

NOW
- Find out how St Bartholomew's Hospital, Bedlam, St Thomas', Christ's Hospital and Bridewell helped poor people in London.

The break with Rome

When Henry VIII came to the throne the people of England and Wales were mainly Roman Catholics.

Henry ordered changes in the Church in England so that it would no longer be ruled from Rome by the Pope.

1. Pope Clement VII, head of the Roman Catholic Church.

2. Thomas Cranmer, Archbishop of Canterbury.

The new Church was described as the Protestant Church.
It had services in English or Welsh. It banned statues and ornaments.

- With a friend, label pictures 1 to 6 either Roman Catholic or Protestant.

3. Henry VIII, head of the Church

4. The Holy Bible (in Latin)

5. The Great Bible (in English)

6. Statue of the Virgin Mary

Picture	Church
1	
2	
3	
4	
5	
6	

NOW
- Find out more about changes in the church.
- Imagine that you are listening to some ordinary Tudor people talking about their parish church. They go to church every Sunday. Some of them like the changes, some do not.
- Write a description of the conversation.
- Give your characters names.

Closing the monasteries

Henry VIII sent visitors to all the monasteries in England and Wales to find out about their land and possessions and to close them.

- Look at the pictures and read the words.

Rievaulx Abbey in Yorkshire. Lead from the roofs was used to make cannonballs. The bells were melted down to make cannons.	People living on monastery land paid tithes (rents) to the monasteries.	It was said that monks and nuns did not live holy lives. Some found work when the monasteries closed. Some were glad of this.
Henry VIII sold monasteries to his courtiers. They were rich enough to convert them into large houses.	Anything that could easily be moved from a monastery became the king's property.	Henry had some rebel abbots hanged.

- Complete the thought bubbles to show what these people might be thinking about Henry VIII's actions.

A farmer on monastery land.

Two monks with different thoughts.

A wealthy courtier.

- What did Henry VIII gain by closing the monasteries?

_____

_____

BRAIN WAVES – Tudor Times

Thomas More

Thomas More was Lord Chancellor from 1529 to 1532. It was during this time that Henry VIII set up the Church of England with himself as its head instead of the Pope.

All my subjects must swear an oath that I am the head of the Church.	 *The Pope is the head of the Church. We cannot take the king's oath.*	*Why will you not swear the oath?*
Some people who took the oath did not really agree with it.	Thomas More and John Fisher, Bishop of Rochester, could not forget their Roman Catholic Faith.	Thomas More stayed silent. He could not lie but did not want to be executed for heresy.
 *Can you not take the oath, yet keep your beliefs?*	 *If you are really the King's loyal servant, why will you not help him?* / *Because the Pope, not the King is the true head of my Church.*	 *I am the King's loyal servant, but God's first.*
He was torn between his conscience and love for his family.	Lord Richard Rich tricked More into giving this answer.	Rich gave evidence at More's trial. More was executed in 1534.

- List some words to describe Thomas More's character.

_____

_____

- Explain your answer to a friend.

- **NOW** Write a letter from Thomas More to his daughter, explaining why he could not agree that Henry was head of the Church.

Edward VI

- Play this game and find out what happened during the reign of Edward VI.
- You need a counter for each player and a dice.

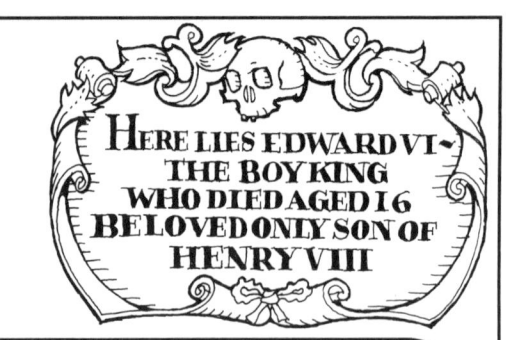

Here lies Edward VI~ The Boy King who died aged 16 Beloved only son of Henry VIII

START ☞	**1547** Edward VI was crowned king at the age of 9. Move on 2 spaces.	**1547** Edward was often ill. Go back to the start.	**1547** The Earl of Hertford made himself Duke of Somerset.
FINISH			**1547** Somerset became Lord Protector to help Edward to rule.
1553 Mary, Edward's sister, came to London with her supporters to claim the throne.			**1549** Somerset led an attack against Scotland. *Go back 1 space.*
1553 Lady Jane Grey was proclaimed queen.			**1549** The Earl of Warwick had Somerset imprisoned in The Tower.
1553 Edward died of consumption. *Go back 4 spaces.*			**1549** Thomas Cranmer wrote the first English Prayer Book. *Move on 2 spaces.*
1553 Northumberland tried to arrange a marriage between his son and Lady Jane Grey.			**1551** Edward said that parts of the prayer book must be re-written to be less Roman Catholic.
1553 Northumberland persuaded Edward to name his cousin, Lady Jane Grey, as the next monarch.	**1553** Edward became very ill. *Go back 3 spaces.*	**1552** Northumberland became Lord Protector.	**1551** The Earl of Warwick became Duke of Northumberland.

BRAIN WAVES – Tudor Times © Folens (copiable page)

Mary I

Mary I was a Roman Catholic.

Her brother, Edward VI and his advisers had been Protestants.

Mary wanted the people of England to follow the Roman Catholic faith.

- Cut out the sentences and stick them in the correct places on this chart.

Protestantism (Edward VI's faith)	Roman Catholicism (Mary I's faith)

- Priests may marry.

- Priests must not marry.

- Church services must be read in Latin.

- Church services can be read in English or Welsh.

- The king or queen is head of the Church.

- The Pope is head of the Church.

- Churches should have statues of the Virgin Mary.

- Churches should not have statues.

NOW
- Find out what Mary did to make England a Roman Catholic country.

Think about ...

- Protestant bishops and priests.
- People who wrote books about Protestant beliefs.
- Priests who were married.
- Ordinary people with Protestant beliefs.

Elizabeth I

From the beginning of her reign, Elizabeth's advisers tried to find a husband for her.

- Read the information on this page. Talk to a friend about why the advisers wanted Elizabeth to marry and why she did not.

I have already in marriage joined myself to a husband, namely the Kingdom of England.

You think if you were married you would be but Queen of England; and now you are King and Queen.

(Sir James Melville)

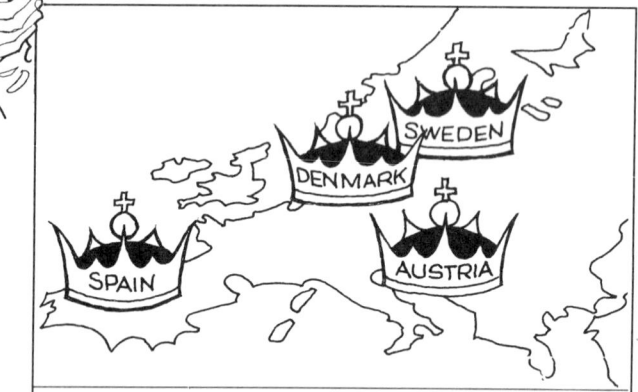

King Phillip of Spain proposed marriage to Elizabeth. So did the King of Denmark, the King of Sweden, Archduke Charles of Austria and many others.

Who will be the next monarch?

There could be problems without a male heir.

The Queen enjoys dancing with her admirers.

- Complete these sentences.
- Elizabeth's advisers wanted her to marry so that:

_____

- Elizabeth refused because:

_____

Bess of Hardwick

START — Bess was born in about 1527 near Chesterfield. Forward two spaces.

In 1528, Bess's father died, and his land was seized by the King. Back two spaces.

In about 1543, Bess married John Barley. Forward one space.

In 1544, John Barley died. Back two spaces.

In 1547, Bess married Sir William Cavendish. Forward one.

- You need a counter for each player and a dice.
- Take turns. Record your scores.
- You must land on FINISH.

Bess of Hardwick

In 1557, Sir William died. Back two.

Edward VI died in 1553 and Mary I was crowned. Forward one.

In 1549, Bess and Sir William bought Chatsworth House in Derbyshire. Forward one.

In 1547, Henry VIII died; Edward VI was crowned.

In 1558 Mary I died, Elizabeth I was crowned. Forward one space.

Hardwick Hall, near Chesterfield, Derbyshire.

In 1560, Bess married William St Loe. Forward one.

In 1565, William St Loe died. Back one.

In 1567 Bess marries the Earl of Shrewsbury. Forward two.

Elizabeth I made the Shrewsburys the guards of Mary, Queen of Scots in 1568. Back two spaces.

Bess organised the building of Hardwick Hall in 1584. Forward two.

- Write some questions about Bess of Hardwick.
- Display the questions for others to answer.
- Bess founded a great dynasty.
- Talk to a friend about what this means.

Elizabeth I died, James I was crowned. Forward one space.

In 1605, Bess's son William was made 1st Duke of Devonshire.

In 1590, the Earl of Shrewsbury died. Back two.

FINISH — Bess died in 1608.

Mary, Queen of Scots

Here is part of Mary's family tree:

```
James IV          =    Margaret Tudor
of Scotland            (sister of Henry VIII)
                │
        ┌───────┴───────┐
   James V         =   Mary
   of Scotland         of Guise
        │
   ┌────┼────────────┐
  James   Robert      Mary           1. Dauphin Francis of France
(died    (died       Queen of Scots = 2. Lord Darnley
 when    when                         3. The Earl of Bothwell
 young)  young)
```

- Cut out and put in order these events in Mary's life:

Mary left Dumbarton for France, to be protected by Henry II of France until she was old enough to marry his son, Francis.	Mary left Scotland for one last time in 1568. She went to England but Elizabeth I asked the Earl of Shrewsbury to guard her.	Mary was crowned Queen of Scotland, in 1543, at the age of nine months.
In 1565, four years after her return to Scotland, Mary married Lord Darnley.	The Earl of Bothwell kidnapped Mary and married her in 1567. The Lords of Scotland imprisoned her.	Mary returned to Scotland in 1561. People cheered when she arrived in Edinburgh.
In 1548 Mary was moved to Dumbarton Castle, which could be guarded against English kidnappers.	Mary married Dauphin Francis in 1558, then became Queen of France when Henry II died in 1559. Francis died in 1560.	Mary, Queen of Scots, was born on 8 December 1542 at Linlithgow Castle in Scotland.
Mary was executed in 1587 at Fotheringay Castle in Northamptonshire.	Scotland became Protestant while Mary was in France. She did not try to change this when she came back, but wanted to worship in private as a Roman Catholic.	Mary and Lord Darnley had a son, James in 1566, the year before Lord Darnley was murdered.

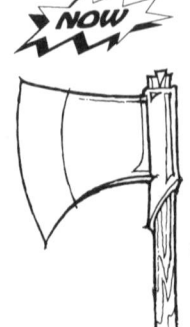

- First Henry VIII, then Elizabeth I worried that Mary could claim the throne of England.
  Explain this. _____
  _____
  _____

- Talk to a friend about the connections between Mary, Queen of Scots and Bess of Hardwick.

Entertaining the Queen

- Imagine that the present queen is coming to stay with you for three days.
Use the chart to plan her visit.

Who will come with her?
Where will everyone sleep and eat?
What will they eat?
What will they do?

Visitors	Where they will sleep	Timetable	
		Mon am	
		pm	
		Tues am	
		pm	
How I will get the house ready		Wed am	
		pm	
		Shopping list	
How I will get myself ready			

Queen Elizabeth I went to stay with important people. She took the people of her court with her. Sometimes over 1000 people went with her on these journeys, called progresses.

NOW

- Find out how some people entertained Queen Elizabeth I and her court.

- Make another planning chart to show how they prepared their homes, how they planned for all these people to sleep and eat and how they entertained them.

© Folens (copiable page)   BRAIN WAVES – *Tudor Times*

Tudor music

Two people can play this game.
How to play:

- Player 1 chooses an instrument card without letting player 2 see it.

- Player 2 asks questions about the instrument.
  The answers can only be 'yes' or 'no'.
  Record the number of questions asked.

- Continue until player 2 finds out which instrument it is.

- Change over and repeat.

- The winner is the player who asks fewest questions.

YOU WILL NEED FOR EACH PLAYER
* TWO COPIES OF THE GAME BOARD, INCLUDING ONE CUT INTO SEPARATE INSTRUMENT CARDS

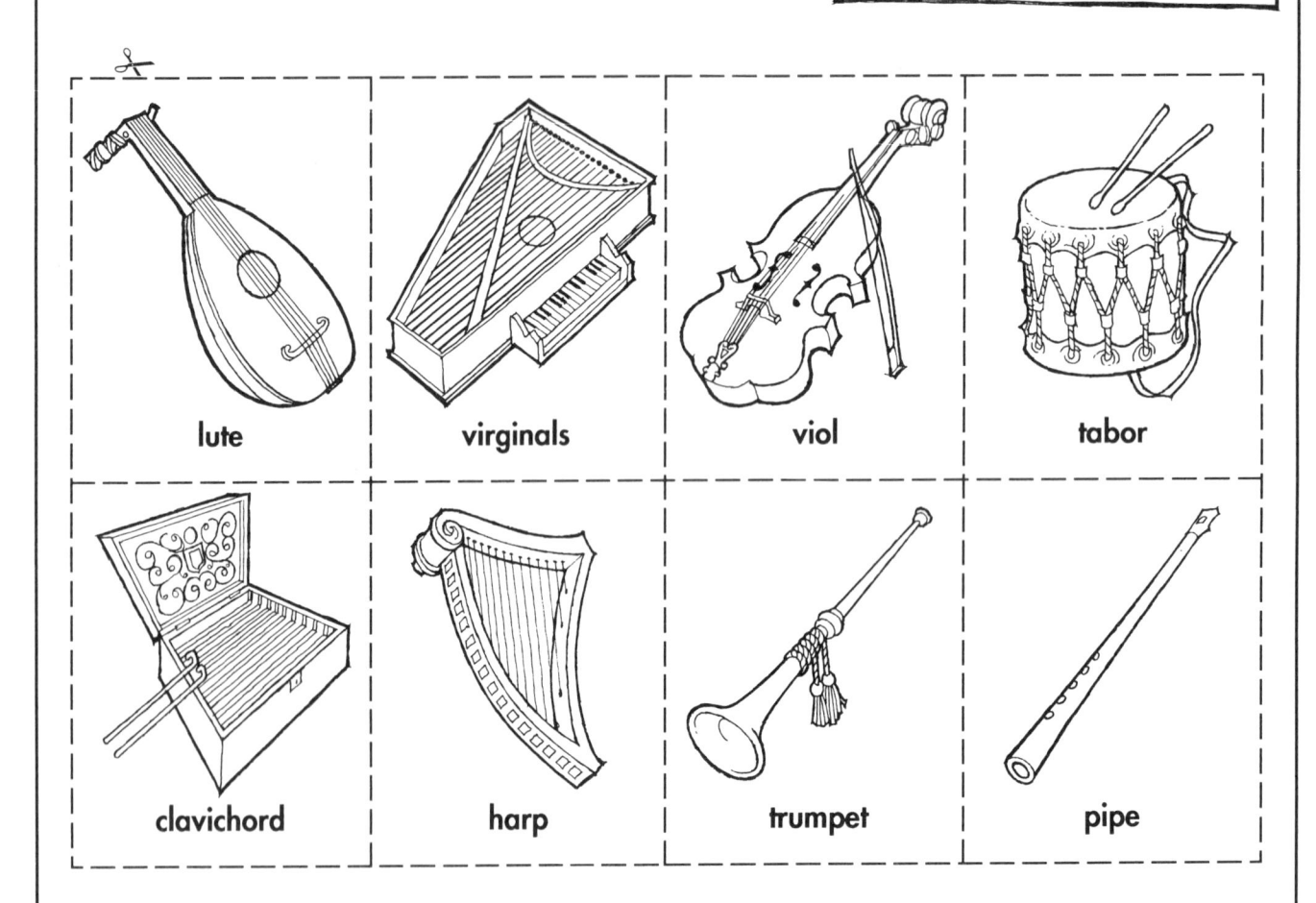

| lute | virginals | viol | tabor |
| clavichord | harp | trumpet | pipe |

- Look at paintings from the time that show these instruments.
- Which present-day instrument is each one like?

Dance: 'Gathering peascods'

This is a 'round dance' for any number of people. It has been simplified here.

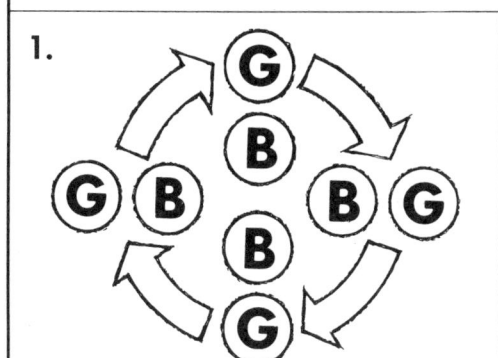

Key: (G) Girl (B) Boy

1. Skip clockwise in a circle in pairs. Repeat this.

2. Repeat 1, but skip anti-clockwise.

3. Boys step to the inside of the circle. Girls step to the outside. Repeat this.

4. Skip clockwise in a circle, this time with everyone linking arms. Repeat this anti-clockwise.

5. Boys join hands and go round on the inside, twice. Girls clap.

6. Girls join hands and go round on the inside. Boys clap.

7. Boys step to the middle and clap. They then step back to their places while the girls step to the middle and clap.

8. Turn on the spot with your partner.

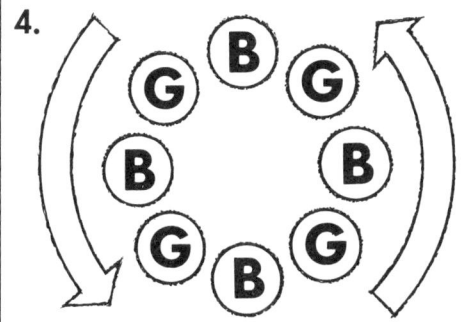

NOW
- Try the whole dance from start to finish, but before you begin, boys bow, girls curtsey.
- Do this again at the end.
- Find some music that matches the dance.

At the table

This is a table set for supper in a wealthy Tudor home.

- Match the labels to the objects.

| wooden trencher or plate | spoon | aquamanile or finger-bowl |

| knife | salt-cellar, just called a 'salt' | wine glass | drinking cup |

- What things are not shown that you might see on a present-day table?

- Explain why an aquamanile was needed.

- Look at paintings from the time to find out more about how people ate and what they ate.

Tudor recipe: cheese tart

Ingredients

Filling
- 225g Cheshire cheese
- 50g butter
- 3 egg yolks

Pastry
- 100g plain flour
- 75g butter
- 1 beaten egg

- Try to read the recipe as it was written in Tudor times:

> 'Take goode fine paste and drive it as thin as you can. Then take cheese, pare it, mince it and bray it in a mortar with the yolks of egs til it be like paste, then put it in a faire dish with clarified butter and then put it abroad into your paste and cover it with a faire cut cover, and so bake it; that doon, serve it forth.'

- Read the recipe in modern English.

Pastry
Turn on the oven (220°C or 425°F), gas mark 7.
Rub the butter into the flour.
Stir in the beaten egg.
Knead the dough.
Roll out just over half the dough.
Grease an ovenproof plate (25cm diameter).
Line the plate with pastry.

Filling
Grate the cheese finely.
Mix together the egg yolks, butter and cheese until they make a smooth paste.
Spread this thickly on the plate.
Roll out the rest of the pastry to make a lid for the pie.
Press down the edges.
Cut two small slits in the pastry lid.
Bake for 15 minutes.

- List the equipment you will need.

_____
_____
_____
_____
_____

- Make the pie.

⚠
- Ask your teacher for permission.
- Be very careful when using the oven.

NOW
- Find out as much as you can about cooking in Tudor times.
- Describe the differences in making this pie then and now.

On the roads

In 1587 William Harrison wrote *A Description of England*. This book helped Elizabeth I to find out about the country's towns, villages, land and roads.

- With a friend, see if you can understand these extracts from Harrison's book.

Glossary

- **amendment** – repair
- **amendeth** – repairs
- **covetous** – envious
- **encroaching** – taking over
- **gulled** – full of gulleys or water channels
- **mire** – mud
- **noisome** – smelly
- **statue** – law
- **travail** – work

1. ... by authority of parliament an order is taken for their (the roads) yearly amendment, whereby all sorts of the common people do employ their travail for six days in the summer upon the same.

   ... such as have land lying upon the sides of the ways do utterly neglect to ditch and scour their drains and water courses.

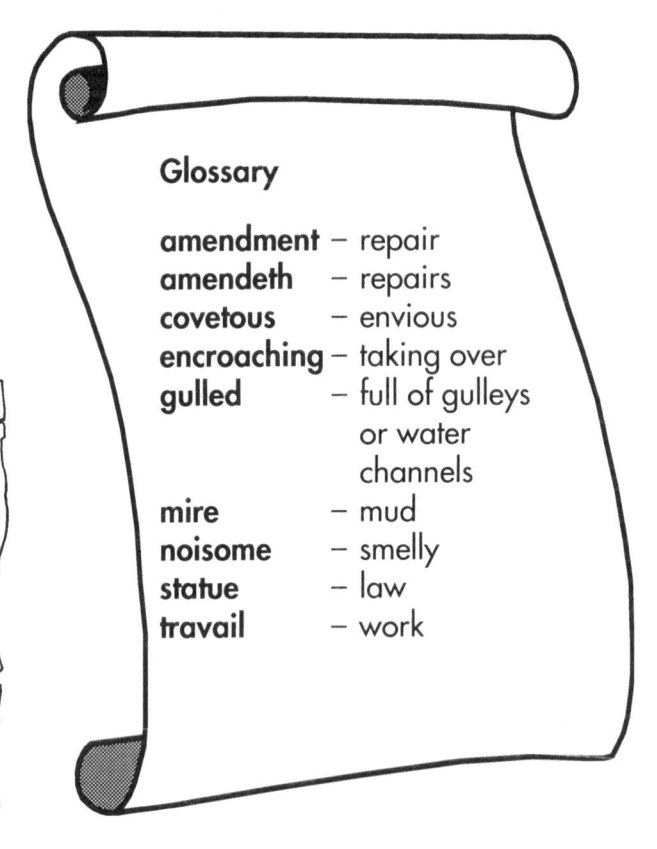

2. Sometimes ... these days' work are not employed upon those ways that lead from market to market, but each surveyor amendeth such by-plots and lanes as seem best for ... easy passage unto his fields and pastures ....

3. ... the streets grow to be much more gulled than before and thereby very noisome for such as travel by the same.

- What did people living near roads have to do to keep them well drained? (1) Did they do this?
- Describe the road surfaces. (3)
- What did the 'common people' have to do to keep the roads in good repair? (1)
- How well did they do this? (2)
- People were supposed to look after roads near to land that they owned. How did they decide which roads to look after? (2)

At sea

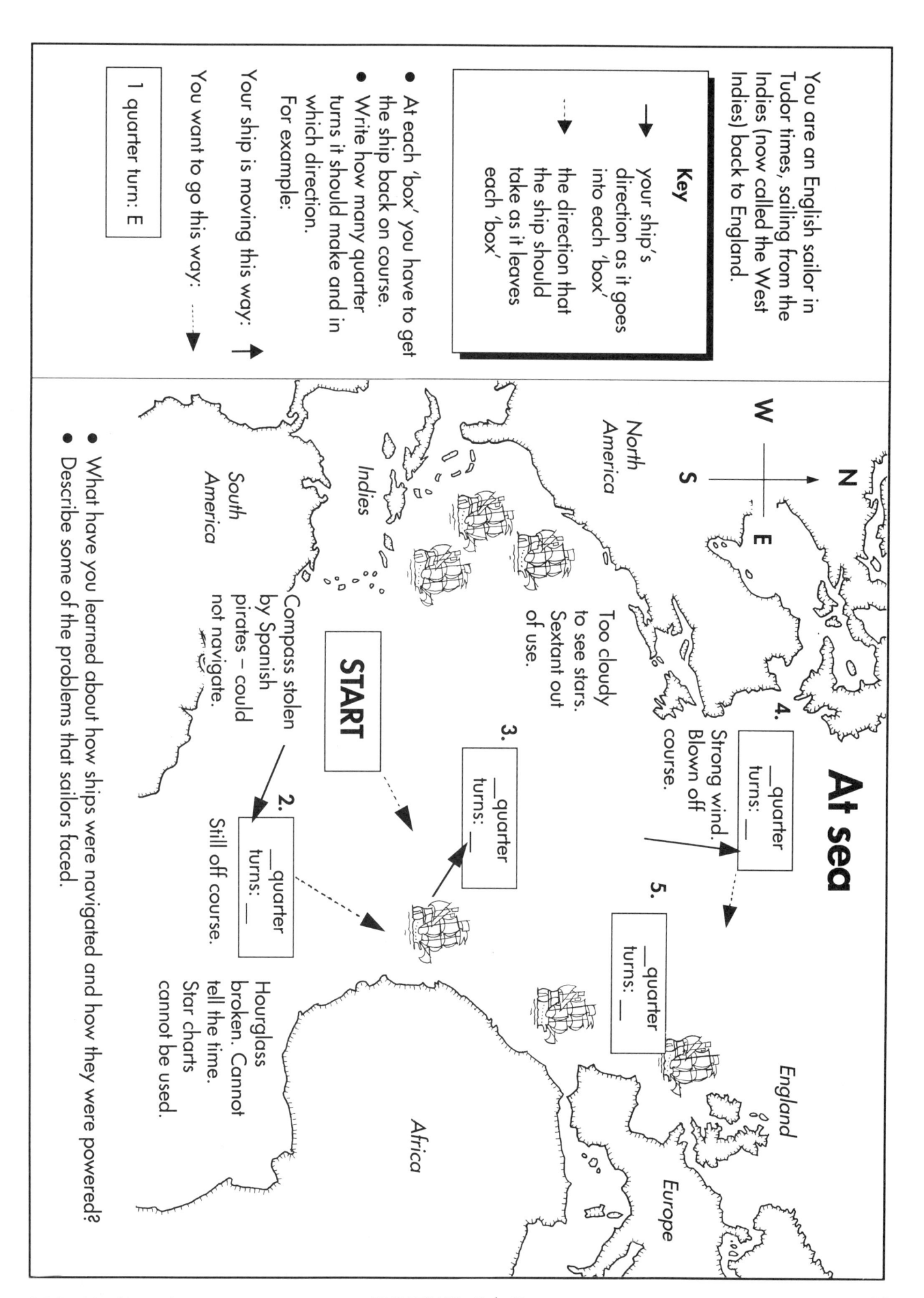

You are an English sailor in Tudor times, sailing from the Indies (now called the West Indies) back to England.

Key
- → your ship's direction as it goes into each 'box'
- ▼ the direction that the ship should take as it leaves each 'box'

- At each 'box' you have to get the ship back on course.
- Write how many quarter turns it should make and in which direction.
  For example:
  Your ship is moving this way: →
  You want to go this way: ▼

  1 quarter turn: E

START — Compass stolen by Spanish pirates – could not navigate.

2. ___ quarter turns: ___ — Still off course.

3. ___ quarter turns: ___ — Too cloudy to see stars. Sextant out of use.

4. ___ quarter turns: ___ — Strong wind. Blown off course.

5. ___ quarter turns: ___ — Hourglass broken. Cannot tell the time. Star charts cannot be used.

Map labels: North America, Indies, South America, Africa, Europe, England

Compass: N, S, E, W

- What have you learned about how ships were navigated and how they were powered?
- Describe some of the problems that sailors faced.

© Folens (copiable page)   BRAIN WAVES – Tudor Times

Adventurers and traders

Tudor monarchs before Elizabeth I had given little attention to exploring and trading overseas, although Henry VIII had built a strong navy.

- What had Tudor monarchs been busy with instead?

Think about the land and farms, the Church, marriage and heirs.

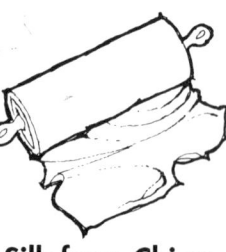

A Tudor ship

Silk from China

People in England could buy goods from many parts of the world but they had to be imported from Spain, Portugal and Italy. These nations had already developed trade routes across the Atlantic to the West Indies, to Africa, China and other parts of the Far East.

Tomatoes from Mexico

The only new routes left to English traders were northwards.

- Read the descriptions of the journeys made northwards to Russia and on to Persia by Anthony Jenkinson.

Spices from the Far East

Sugar from the West Indies

- Estimate how far he and his crew travelled: _____ km.

They sailed from England, across the North Sea, around the north coast of Norway and Finland, to the Russian port of Archangel. They sailed down the river Dvina to Moscow, then: 'The eighth day we came unto a fair town called Murom ... the eleventh day we came to ... Nijni Novgorod, situated at the falling of the river Oka into the worthy River Volga.'

They passed Kazan and:
'... by a goodly river called Kama, unto Astrakhan, and so following the north and north east side of the Caspian Sea to a land of Tartars called Turkmen ...'

Then they travelled on land, by camel, through Uzbek, to the east of the Caspian Sea.

NOW
- Draw Jenkinson's route on the map (page 35).
- Find out about the travels of other explorers and traders.
  Use a different colour to draw each route.

Sea routes

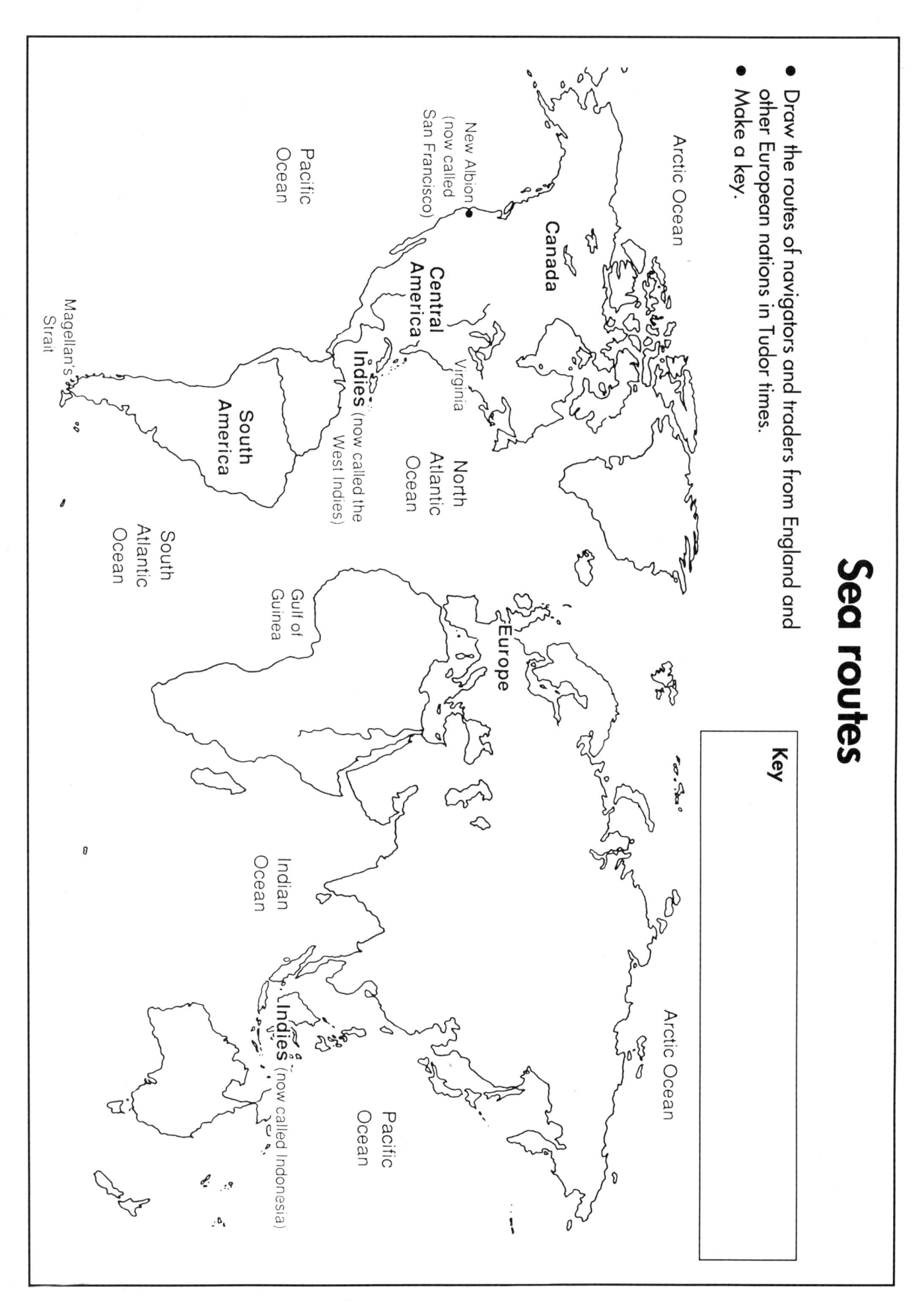

- Draw the routes of navigators and traders from England and other European nations in Tudor times.
- Make a key.

Labels on map:

- Arctic Ocean
- Canada
- New Albion (now called San Francisco)
- Pacific Ocean
- Central America
- Indies (now called the West Indies)
- Virginia
- North Atlantic Ocean
- South America
- Magellan's Strait
- South Atlantic Ocean
- Gulf of Guinea
- Europe
- Indian Ocean
- Indies (now called Indonesia)
- Pacific Ocean
- Arctic Ocean

Key

© Folens (copiable page)   BRAIN WAVES – Tudor Times

The quarrel with Spain

A Elizabeth I

B Phillip II of Spain

C Sir Francis Drake

D Robert Dudley, Earl of Leicester

E William Cecil, Lord Burghley

F Pope Sixtus V

England and Spain had not been on friendly terms for some time. Phillip II of Spain wanted to spread Roman Catholicism through Europe. He had been married to Mary I of England, who was a Roman Catholic. Phillip ruled parts of the Netherlands, where Protestants were rebelling.

Elizabeth I was a Protestant. She sent the Earl of Leicester with his army to defend the Dutch ports of Brill and Flushing from the Spaniards.

Elizabeth commanded Sir Francis Drake to sail to the Spanish port of Cadiz to destroy as many ships as possible. Her Secretary of State, Lord Burghley, had persuaded her to have Mary, Queen of Scots, executed.

- Match the words to the people in the pictures.

1 I will answer your requests after you have conquered England.

2 You must sign the warrant for Mary, Queen of Scots to be executed. She is plotting to take the throne.

3 I entreat you to make a declaration that I should rule England if Mary, Queen of Scots does not succeed Elizabeth. My claim is that I was once joint ruler of England, as husband of Mary I.

4 I could set up an English colony around Brill and Flushing. I could become its governor.

5 Allow me to help you to keep the Spanish out. I can send armies to defend your ports.

6 I have destroyed the Santa Cruz, the galleon of the Spanish admiral.

- Explain why Elizabeth I wanted to send armies to Brill and Flushing.

_____
_____

- Did Elizabeth I want a war with Spain, or did she just try to defend England? Explain your answer.

_____
_____

The Spanish Armada

- With a friend, read this 'fact file'.
- Decide why Phillip of Spain sent the Duke of Medina Sidonia with the Armada to attack England.

1553 Mary I, a Catholic, married Phillip II of Spain, who was also a Catholic.

1558 Mary I died, the Protestant Elizabeth I became Queen of England. She later refused to marry Phillip II.

From 1559 Francis Drake, John Hawkins and other adventurers started to attack Spanish ships. In 1586 Drake raided Spanish land in the West Indies.

1579 Spain helped Catholics in Ireland to rebel against English rule. In 1584 the Spanish ambassador in England was accused of plotting to help Mary, Queen of Scots become Queen of England and was sent to Spain.

1585 Elizabeth I sent troops to the Netherlands to help the Dutch Protestants against the Spaniards.

1587 Mary, Queen of Scots, who was Roman Catholic, was executed. Drake's fleet destroyed Spanish ships at Cadiz in Spain.

- Imagine you are Phillip II of Spain. Explain why you are going to attack England.

_____
_____
_____
_____

Printing: Tudor bestsellers

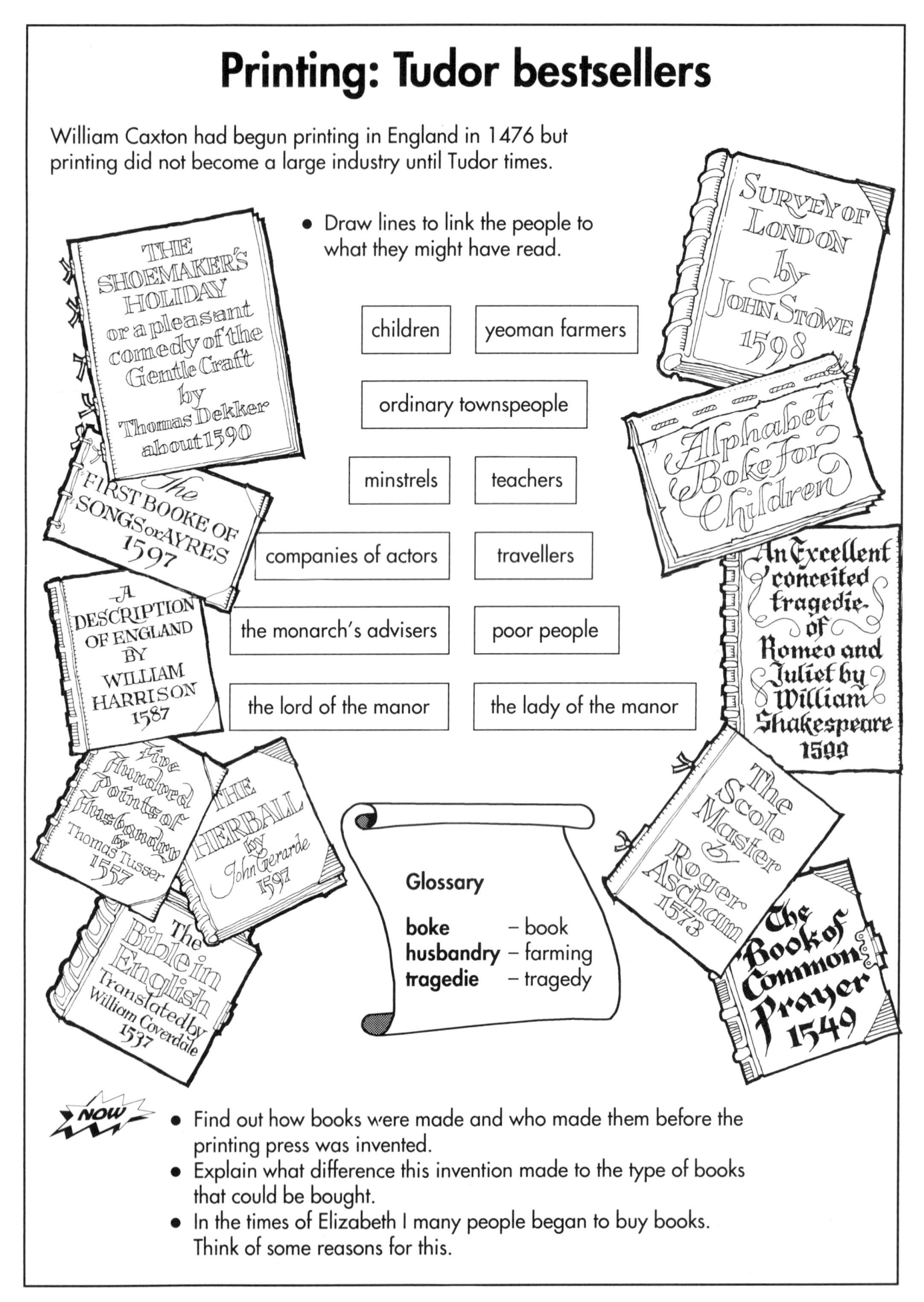

William Caxton had begun printing in England in 1476 but printing did not become a large industry until Tudor times.

- Draw lines to link the people to what they might have read.

Books shown:
- THE SHOEMAKER'S HOLIDAY or a pleasant comedy of the Gentle Craft by Thomas Dekker about 1590
- The First Booke of Songs or Ayres 1597
- A Description of England by William Harrison 1587
- Five Hundred Points of Husbandry by Thomas Tusser 1557
- The Herball by John Gerarde 1597
- The Bible in English Translated by William Coverdale 1537
- Survey of London by John Stowe 1598
- Alphabet Boke for Children
- An Excellent conceited tragedie of Romeo and Juliet by William Shakespeare 1599
- The Scole Master by Roger Ascham 1573
- The Book of Common Prayer 1549

People:
- children
- yeoman farmers
- ordinary townspeople
- minstrels
- teachers
- companies of actors
- travellers
- the monarch's advisers
- poor people
- the lord of the manor
- the lady of the manor

Glossary

- **boke** – book
- **husbandry** – farming
- **tragedie** – tragedy

NOW
- Find out how books were made and who made them before the printing press was invented.
- Explain what difference this invention made to the type of books that could be bought.
- In the times of Elizabeth I many people began to buy books. Think of some reasons for this.

Going to school in 1557

- Talk to a friend about all the things that you have to remember:
  - to do before you go to school
  - to take to school
  - to behave well.

- List these things:

Do before school	Take to school	Behaviour

A A horn book

- With a friend, read source **B**: advice to schoolchildren in 1557.
  Circle anything on your list that is similar to this advice.
  Circle things in source **B** that would be good advice to children today.

B

Thy hands se thou washe, and thy head keame,
And of thy rayment se torne be no seame
Thy cappe fayre brusht thy hed cover than
Takying it of in speaking to any man ...

A napkyn se that thou have in redines
Thy nose to clense from all fylthines.
Thy nayles, yf nede be se that thou payre
Thyne eares kepe clene, thy teath washe thou fayre.

This done, thy setchell and thy bokes take
And to the scole haste se thou make.
But ere thou go with thyselfe forthynke
That thou take with thee pen, paper and ynke.

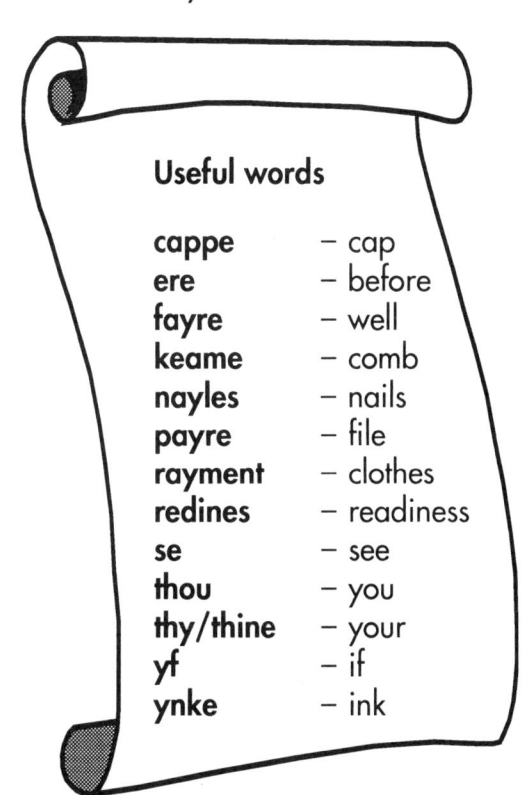

Useful words

cappe	– cap
ere	– before
fayre	– well
keame	– comb
nayles	– nails
payre	– file
rayment	– clothes
redines	– readiness
se	– see
thou	– you
thy/thine	– your
yf	– if
ynke	– ink

NOW • What do the sources on this page tell you about the things that children had to learn in 1557?

Shovelboard

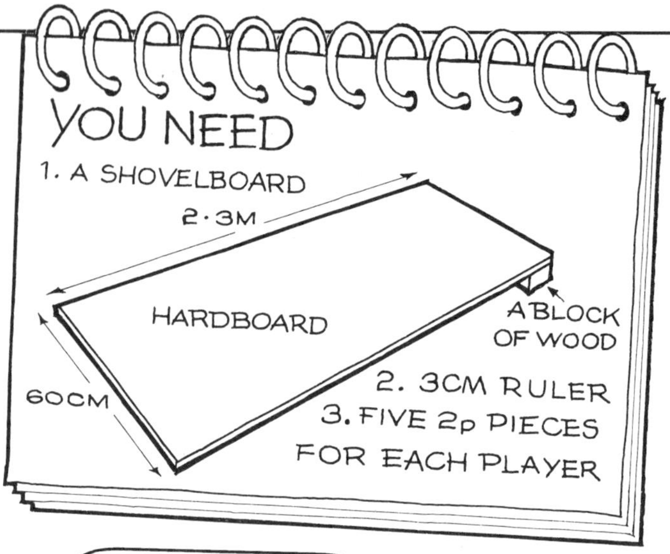

An inventory dated 1600 from Ingatestone Hall in Essex lists 'an old shovelaboard'.

- Mark out your board like this:

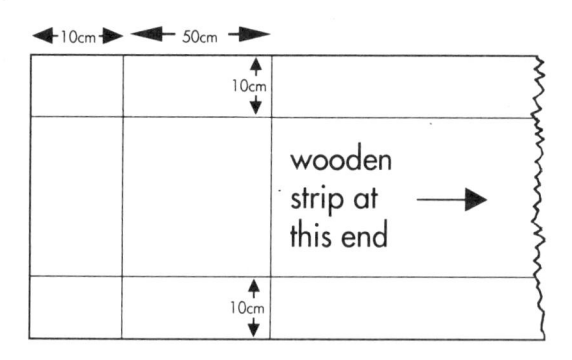

YOU NEED
1. A SHOVELBOARD — 2.3M × 60CM HARDBOARD, A BLOCK OF WOOD
2. 3CM RULER
3. FIVE 2p PIECES FOR EACH PLAYER

Two people can play. Take turns to hit a coin, like this:

HIT DON'T SCRAPE

One player has 'heads' the other has 'tails'.

Do not score until all coins have been played.

- Keep score:

  ● 3 pts   ◉ 2 pts   ○ 1 pt

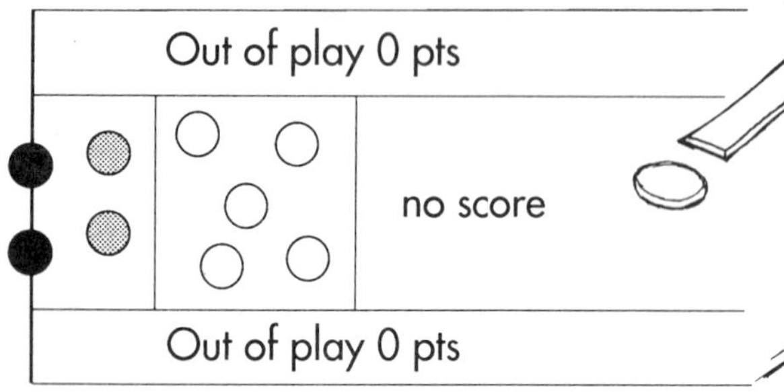

  Out of play 0 pts

  no score

  Out of play 0 pts

SHOVELBOARD
WOODEN FLAP TO STOP BOARD SLIPPING
TABLE TOP

Rules

All coins are left on the board until the end of the round (when all coins have been played), except:
- (a) those more than half over the 'out of play' lines and, of course,
- (b) those that have been knocked off the table.

You can knock your opponent's coins off the table.

Scoreboard

Game	Players' names	
1		
2		
3		
4		
5		

Sports and games

A.

In 1487 Parliament said that England's defence depended on skill with longbows, but that men were losing this skill because crossbows were becoming popular.

They passed an Act that said no longbow should be sold for more than 3s 4d (17p).

In 1512 people were spending little time on archery because they were enjoying other games, like those on this page.

B.

- Why did Parliament want longbows to be cheap?

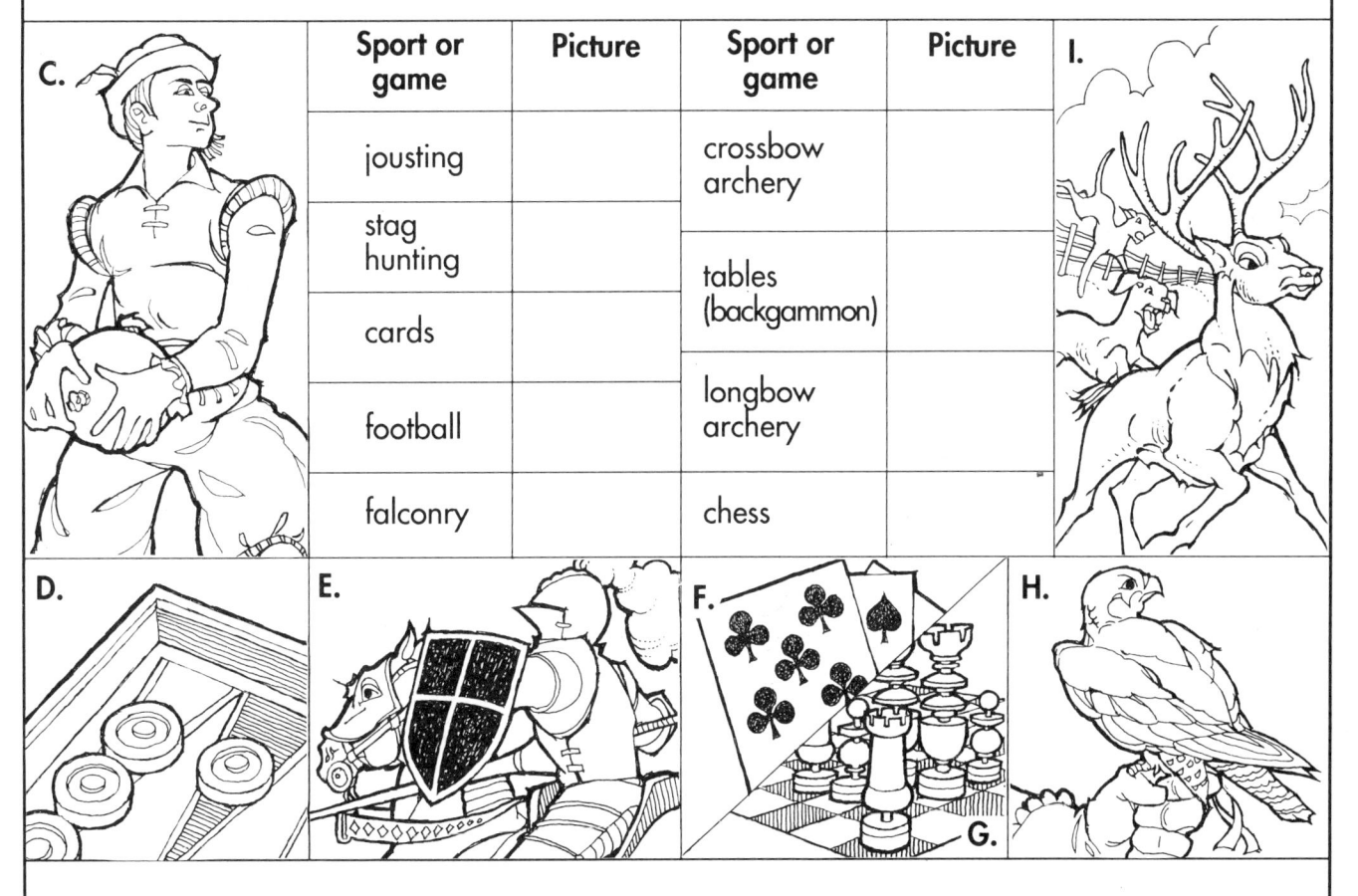

- Match the headings to the sports or games.

Sport or game	Picture	Sport or game	Picture
jousting		crossbow archery	
stag hunting		tables (backgammon)	
cards			
football		longbow archery	
falconry		chess	

C. D. E. F. G. H. I.

- Find out about other sports and games that people played in Tudor times.
- Find out what Parliament did in 1512 to make sure that men practised archery.

A manor house

Ingatestone Hall was built in about 1540. Sir William and Lady Anne Petre and their family lived there.

The plan shows the ground floor in 1600.

KEY
- **1–3.** Low chamber rooms
- **4.** Stool house
- **5.** Dining parlour
- **6.** Pantry
- **7.** Beer and wine cellars
- **8–11.** Corner chambers with stool house
- **12.** Entry into the orchard
- **13.** Chapel
- **14, 15, 18, 19.** Chamber rooms
- **16.** Nursery
- **17.** Maids' inner room
- **20.** Entry to kitchen yard
- **21–25.** Larders, salt house and scullery
- **26–29.** Kitchen, buttery and beer cellar
- **30–31.** Hall and porch

- Talk to a friend about what you can find out about life at Ingatestone Hall in Tudor times.

- Which food and drinks were stored in large amounts?

  _____
  _____
  _____

- Explain why these foods were stored.

  _____
  _____

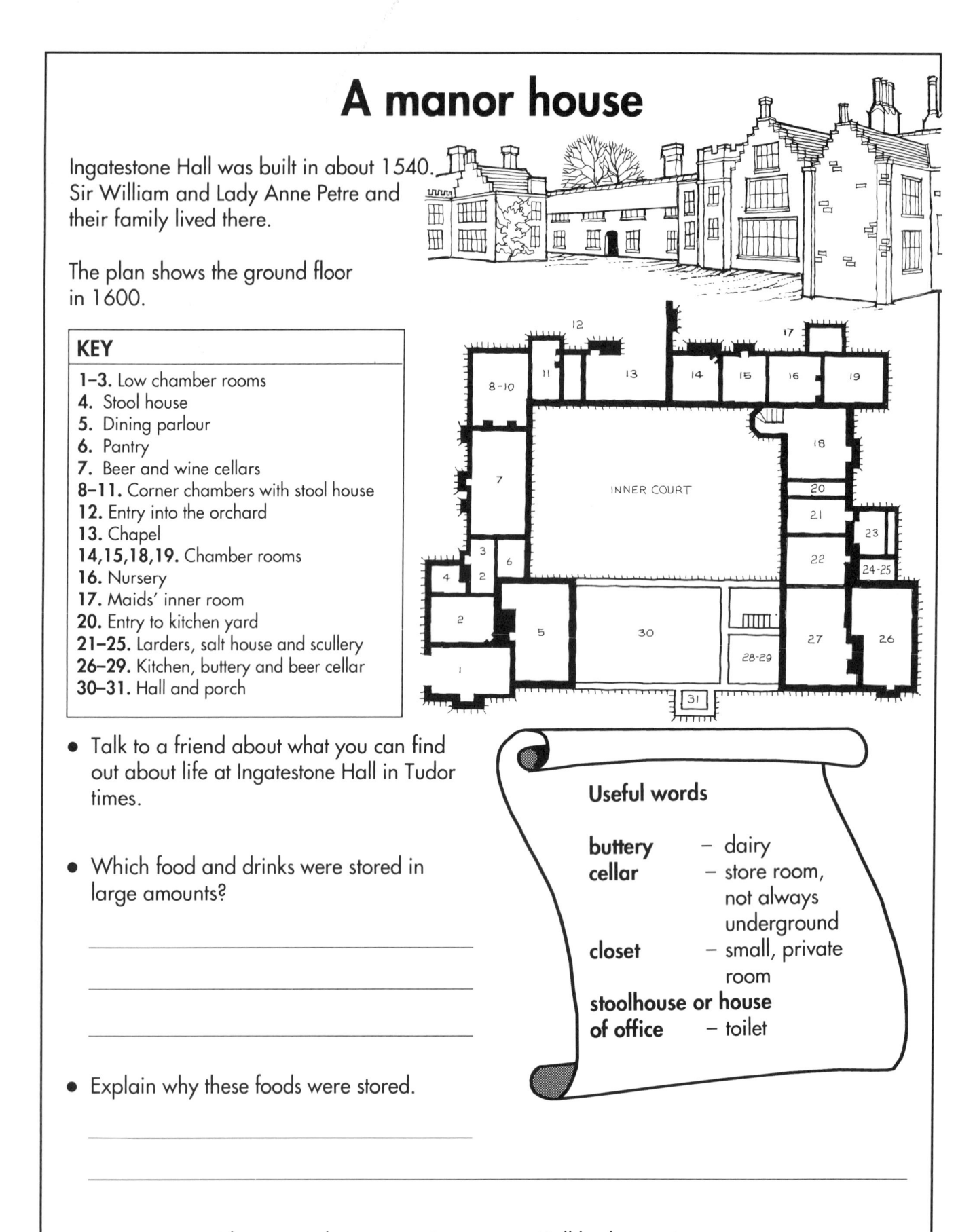

Useful words

- **buttery** – dairy
- **cellar** – store room, not always underground
- **closet** – small, private room
- **stoolhouse or house of office** – toilet

NOW
- Like many other manors Ingatestone Hall had, upstairs, an armoury and a long gallery.
- Find out what these were used for.

The great chamber

The lord and lady of the manor would sit and talk to visitors in the great chamber.

- Ring the artefacts in this chamber that do not belong to Tudor times.

- Explain why these artefacts do not belong.

_____ _____
_____ _____
_____ _____
_____ _____
_____ _____
_____ _____
_____ _____
_____ _____
_____ _____
_____ _____

> **NOW** • Look at paintings from the time to find out more about Tudor furniture and artefacts.

An ordinary home

This is the home of Alexander Paramore, a farmer in Kent. The furniture and other household things are listed.

Bedroom 2
a flock bed
2 chests
2 spinning wheels
a flour bin
2 tubs

Bedroom 1
2 feather beds
2 linen chests

Hall
a painted cloth
a wooden table
a wooden chair
a wooden bench
pewter dishes
tin spoons
3 pewter candlesticks

Kitchen
2 kettles
2 iron pans
3 brass pots
2 spits
1 dripping pan
dairy vessels
brewing equipment

- Discuss these questions with a friend.

> How did the Paramore family light their home?

> Where did they eat?

> Where did they keep their clothes?

> How did they cook?

- List some things that were made in the farm house:

_____
_____

- List some questions about ordinary Tudor people at home:

_____
_____
_____
_____

> How did they wash?

> How did they clean their houses?

NOW • Use pictures and written sources to answer the questions.

44 BRAIN WAVES – *Tudor Times* © Folens (copiable page)

Keeping healthy

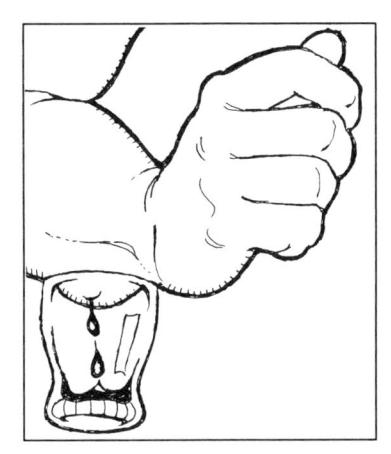

We can find out, from books written at the time, what sort of advice was given to people to keep healthy.

People in England still believed in the Mediaeval idea of the four humours or fluids in the body.

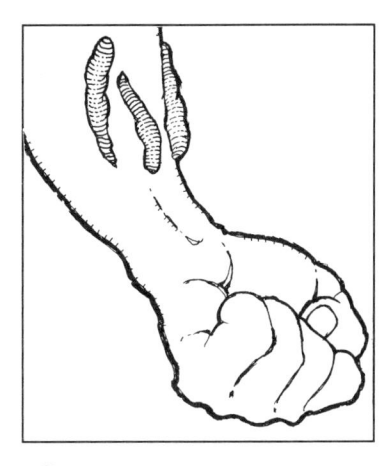

A Cupping glasses were used to let out blood.

B Leeches were used to suck out blood.

C There is nothing that comforts the heart as much as honest mirth and good company. A small amount of wine lightens the heart and good bread keeps the heart healthy. Other good drinks comfort the heart and make good blood. Sweet things, mace and ginger, raw and softly poached eggs are good.

From *A Breviary of Helthe* by Andrewe Boord (1547) – changed here to present-day English.

D The four humours or fluids of the body:
- sanguine (blood)
- phlegm
- choler (bile)
- melancholy.

A healthy person had the right amount of all humours. (A present-day interpretation.)

- Explain why doctors used cupping glasses or leeches to let out blood.

E Old people are phlegmatic (cold and moist), so should not eat lamb. Children are phlegmatic and should have hot, moist diets. As they grow up they become sanguine or choleric and can eat red meat and salads. All fruits are bad for people. They cause bad humours. Milk is good for students because they are often melancholic.

From *Castle of Health* by Thomas Elyot (1541) – changed here to present-day English.

F Eggs are good. The following harm the eyesight: leeks, onions, garlic, pepper, beans, lentils, wine, tears, wind, bright sunshine and baths.

A modern interpretation of an old poem that many Tudor doctors believed.

- Make a chart to show how sources **C**, **E** and **F** disagree.

- **NOW**
  - Read different present-day sources that give advice about health.
  - Show on a chart how they agree or disagree.
  - Compare them with Tudor advice about health.

Source			
Food	C	E	F
eggs	good		good
wine			
sweet things			

Clothes for a nobleman (1500)

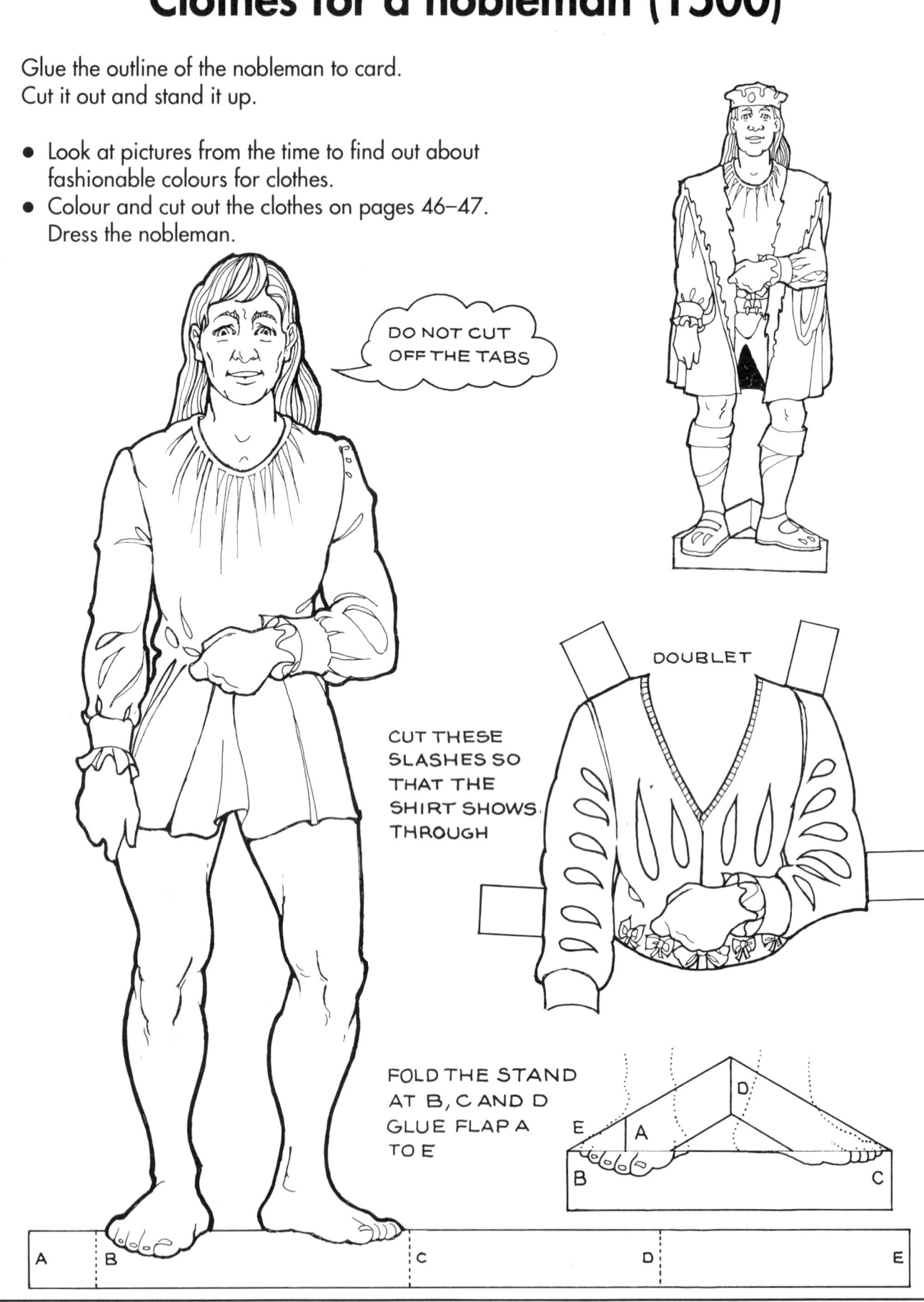

Glue the outline of the nobleman to card.
Cut it out and stand it up.

- Look at pictures from the time to find out about fashionable colours for clothes.
- Colour and cut out the clothes on pages 46–47. Dress the nobleman.

DO NOT CUT OFF THE TABS

DOUBLET

CUT THESE SLASHES SO THAT THE SHIRT SHOWS THROUGH

FOLD THE STAND AT B, C AND D GLUE FLAP A TO E

Clothes for a nobleman (1500)

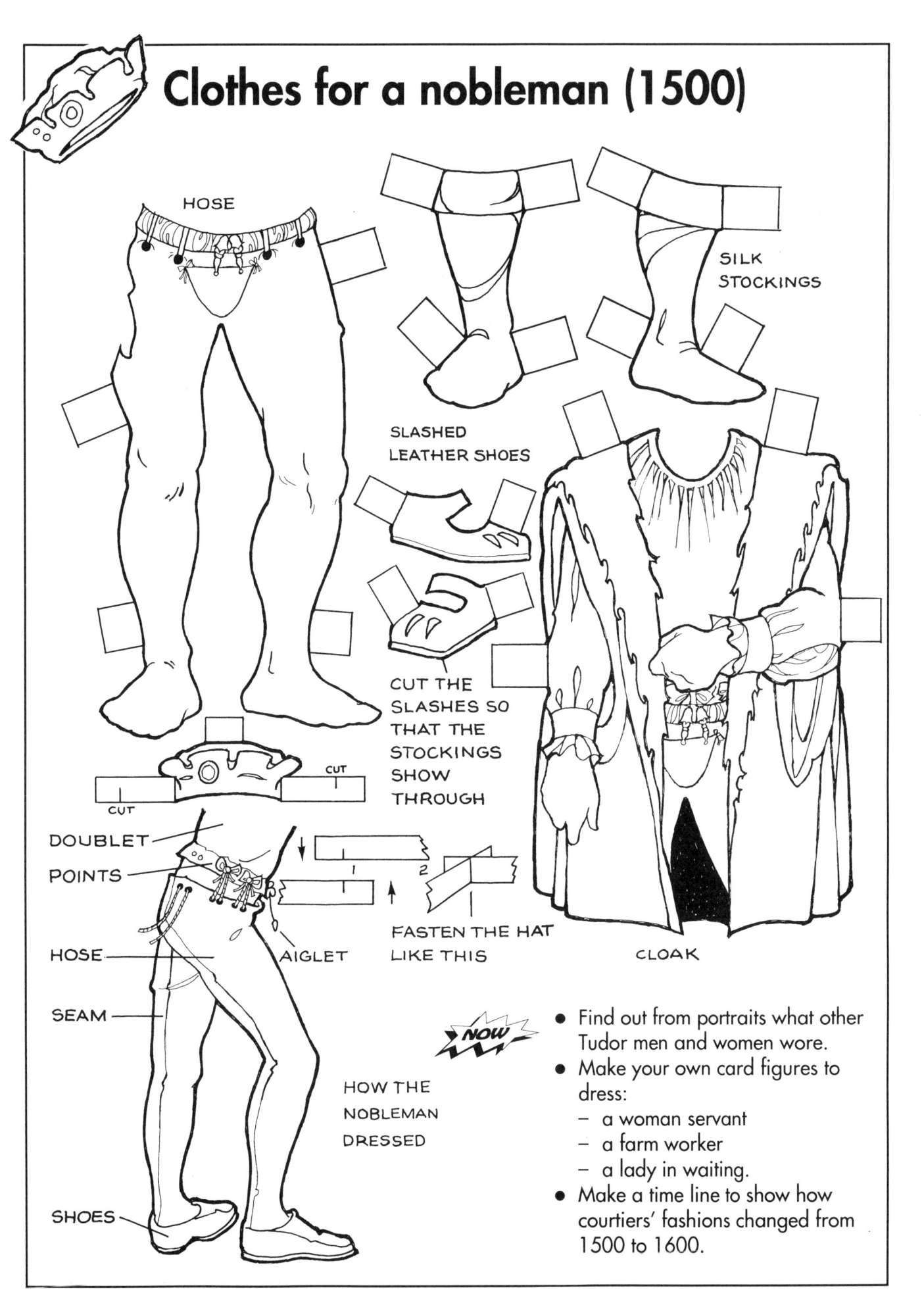

HOSE

SILK STOCKINGS

SLASHED LEATHER SHOES

CUT THE SLASHES SO THAT THE STOCKINGS SHOW THROUGH

CUT

CUT

DOUBLET
POINTS

HOSE
AIGLET

SEAM

FASTEN THE HAT LIKE THIS

CLOAK

SHOES

HOW THE NOBLEMAN DRESSED

NOW
- Find out from portraits what other Tudor men and women wore.
- Make your own card figures to dress:
  - a woman servant
  - a farm worker
  - a lady in waiting.
- Make a time line to show how courtiers' fashions changed from 1500 to 1600.

© Folens (copiable page) BRAIN WAVES – Tudor Times

A Tudor comedy

The play *Gamer Gurton's Nedle* was written in 1575, probably by William Stevenson. It was meant to make people laugh.

- Read the part of the play shown in the pictures.
- Draw the next two pictures and write in the speech bubbles.

Glossary

breeches	– type of short trousers worn over hose
Gamer	– Grandma
nedle	– needle
thou sawest	– you saw
thus	– like this

Panel 1: GAMER GURTON: "Out thief!" (GYB THE CAT at milk)

Panel 2: "Alas, Hodge, alas, I may well curse this day that I ever saw it, with Gyb and the milk." (HODGE THE SERVANT)

Gamer Gurton went on to tell Hodge about her lost needle.

Panel 3: "Didst carry out the dust – seek where thou pourest it down. And as thou sawest me raking in the ashes. So see in all the heap of dust. Leave no straw unturned." (TYB THE MAID)

Off went Tyb to search through all the dust.

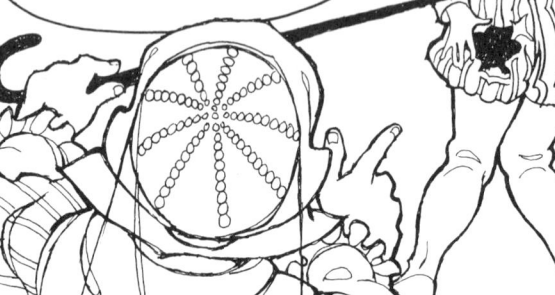

Panel 4: "Your nedle is lost, it is a pity you should lack care. How will you sew my breeches? Shall I go out thus tomorrow?"

NOW
- With friends, enact this part of the play.
- Continue the play using the scenes below, making it as funny as you can.
- Hodge searched in the flour and the ashes in the fireplace. He rushed towards something shining in a corner, but it was only Gyp's eyes.
- Gamer Gurton prayed to St Ostyth to send back the needle. Hodge told her how careless she was since she had nothing else to do but sew.
- Gamer's son Cocke arrived. She told him to look in an old shoe for a candle, light the candle and look for the needle. Gamer told him how useless he was.